Rockhound and Prospector magazine

Spring 2023

Treasures from the sand and sea!

Shell collecting
With Jamie from plum island
Sea cabins

Ethical seashell Collecting
with Sharmon from
Swf Beach life

The wonders of Sea glass
With Author
Mary Beth Beuke

Agates
Along Lake Superior

Fossil treasures
With
Charleston Fossil
Adventures

Fresh water pearls
With Ashley McNamara

Summer 2023

ROCKHOUND AND PROSPECTOR MAGAZINE

CONTENTS

GEMS * ROCKS* FOSSILS * PROSPECTING

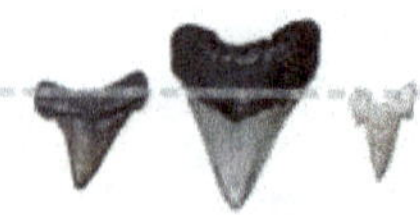
ROCKHOUNDMAGAZINE@YAHOO.COM

Rockhound and prospector Magazine

Event listing 25.00

Advertising rates

Full page w/ color 250.00
1/2 Page w/color 200.00
1/4 page w/color 150.00

trade negotiation of goods for advertising space possible

www.https://shetannoir.wixsite.com/ squatchgqmagazine

Rockhoundmagazine@yahoo.com

Published by Squatch GQ magazine llc
Owner Shetan Noir
Editor-in-chief: Shetan Noir

Charleston Fossil Adventures

By Shetan Noir

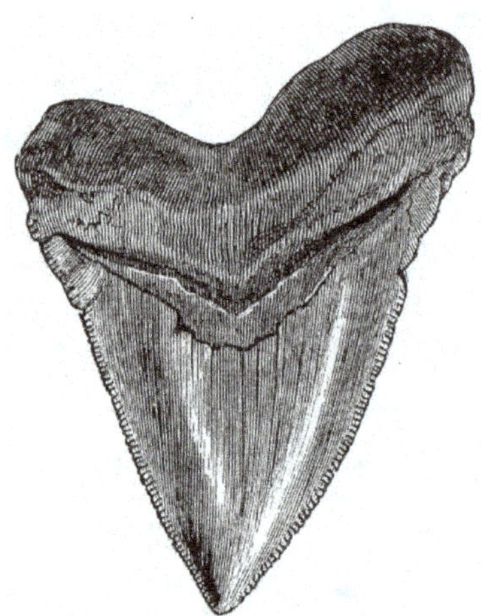

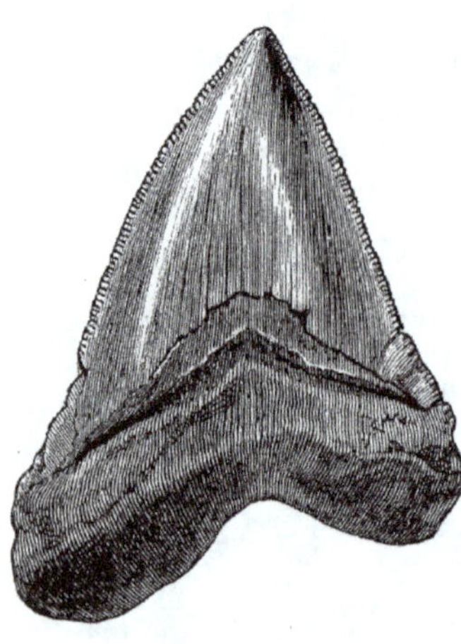

How did you become a paleontologist?

I received my degree from Appalachian State University. You can pursue a few different fields and still wind up within paleontology; biology, environmental science, evolutionary biology, and geology are all degrees that can lead to paleontology as a profession. My degree is in environmental science. Following graduation I worked at a state park in South Carolina as the interpretive ranger, and curated their fossil collection and museum for three

.

Can you tell us more about your different fossil collecting tours?

We offer Fossil Adventures in increments of 2, 4, and 6 hours, geared towards beginner, intermediate, and advanced fossil collectors. These Adventures are listed on our website as the "1 Island Adventure, 2 Island Adventure, and 3 Island Adventure" where we visit, you guessed it -- 1, 2, and 3 islands, respectively. Our fourth offering is called the Prehistoric Plantation Cruise where we take clients past four of Charleston's historic plantations, and explain the link between post-Civil War prosperity in the south and paleontology. Charleston was once the world's largest producer of phosphate fertilizer, and this industry provided the cash injection our economy needed to rebuild from the destruction of the Civil War.

What can people expect on your tours, Can you tell us what a tour involves?

During the 1, 2, and 3 Island Adventures, clients are taken by boat to secluded shorelines that yield fossils dating back 30 million years. At the site, we simply scan the surface with our eyes to locate common and unusual fossils from the Ice Age and beyond. Believe it or not, incredible fossils wash out every day at these sites, with no sign of diminishing any time soon! We hunt the shorelines of dredge islands from the early 20th Century. During the historic dredging operations, machinery dug down into fossiliferous layers laden with shark teeth, whale bones, sea turtle fossils, and more. Now, thanks to currents from the rivers, prehistoric remains wash out with each retreating tide. During the tour we provide knee pads as well as collection aprons that our clients get to keep after their Adventure. At the end of our 2 and 3 Island Adventures, Ashby sits down with each client and sorts all of their fossils into categories according to the animal species and bone type. Following this sorting, our clients are invited to film Ashby as he narrates in great detail what the guests have found and what makes some specimens more unusual than others.

What types of fossils and teeth do you commonly find on your tours?

Fossils found in the South Carolina Lowcountry date back 30 million years. Our oldest deposits are marine layers containing fossils from toothed echolocating dolphins, leatherback and loggerhead sea turtles, a false-toothed bird with a 30-foot wingspan (*Pelagornis*) saltwater crocodiles, early sirenians (manatee & dugong relatives) sawfish, and of course lots and lots of sharks. Charleston offers a wonderful glimpse at our Oligocene oceans, and as such, one of the shark teeth we find most commonly on our tours is from *Carcharocles/Otodus angustidens*, aka megalodon's "grandfather", two species prior to the evolution of megalodon. Ice Age fossils we often find are teeth from bison, horses, armoring from giant armadillos, giant sloth teeth, semi-aquatic turtle shell, camel, and even rhinoceros remains!

What tips do you suggest for a successful fossil collecting trip?

First and foremost, a positive attitude! Coming in with unrealistic expectations is guaranteed to provide a let down when that 7" megalodon tooth didn't wash out. More practically, wearing closed-toe footwear, staying hydrated, and bringing your prescription glasses or readers to be able to spot smaller fossils or patterns are all key.

Do guests get to keep everything they find?

Absolutely! Unless we see any specimen that is scientifically significant and warrants donation, guests are allowed to keep all finds. Don't worry, this means you get to keep all of those shark teeth!

Are there any laws or rules about collecting fossils from the water or beaches? Do you need a permit?

Yes. The 1991 SC Antiquities Act protects all fossils and human artifacts older than 50 years that are found in our waterways. Any individual looking to hunt underwater is required to have a "Hobby Diving License" for the collection of these remains. This license should be called an artifact collection license, as it is required in any navigable waterway, regardless of if you are diving or not. Individuals with this license are not allowed to use tools of any kind, and must report their finds quarterly to the state. If, after 60 days, the state does not want anything collected, the individual is free to sell, keep, or otherwise distribute the artifacts they found. Beaches and shorelines do not fall under this law as fossils are *ex situ*, or, taken out of geologic context and of less scientific significance.
You also wrote a book about fossil collecting, Can you tell us more about it?

In 2020 my parents and I published *A Beachcomber's Guide to Fossils* through the University of Georgia Press. We worked for six years on completing the text, which has over 1200 full color images, 325+ fossils described, and a range applicable in the US from Texas east to Florida, and north to New Jersey. The temporal range is primarily from the Paleocene through the Pleistocene, although some older specimens are included. The book is presented in field guide format, sized 6x9 inches, and with 544 pages. Interspersed throughout the book are 12 "Species Highlights" where we cover the history of different animal lineages. We wrote the book in an approachable style, as a bridge between dry academic texts and the general public who genuinely want to learn more about our planet. To facilitate this approach, at the bottom of each identification page we've included fun facts and humour to lighten the more technical information above. Even if people only buy the book for the photos, they'll gain a greater understanding of what to look for when combing a beach.

Is there anything else you want to tell us about your fossil collecting tours?

CFA has operated legally and ethically within state regulations since its founding in 2016. We take great pride in our approach to educating the public, protecting the environment, and facilitating the donation of scientifically significant finds to local museums and institutions.
Do you have any social media sites or websites?

You can find us online at chsfossiladventures.com, on Facebook at "Charleston Fossil Adventures," and view videos from our trips on YouTube at "Charleston Fossil Adventures." We also have a Patreon account under the business name for the fossil identification services we provide.

Thanks for featuring CFA in the issues of these magazines! I look forward to seeing each issue.

Also, could you please send a complimentary copy of each magazine to the following address? Thanks!

Charleston Fossil Adventures

9544 Koester Rd

Ladson, SC 29456

A BEACHCOMBER'S GUIDE TO
FOSSILS
Bob Gale / Pam Gale / Ashby Gale
Photography by Ashby Gale   With a foreword by Rudy Mancke

58th Annual

GEM MINERAL
FOSSIL SHOW

Sponsored by Lawrence County Rock Club, Inc.

Website: www.lawrencecountyrockclub.org

JUNE 23, 24 & 25, 2023

PUBLIC INVITED

Wide Variety of Gems, Jewelry, Beads, Minerals, Fossils, Rocks, Gifts, Lapidary Supplies, Rockhound & Prospecting Supplies, 4-H Project Material, Science Project Material

Show Schedule- EDT

Friday 23rd 10:00 AM to 6:30 PM

Saturday 24th 9:00 AM to 6:30 PM

Sunday 25th 10:00 AM to 4:00 PM

Saturday 24th

I.S.P. – INDIANA SOCIETY OF PALEONTOLOGY – 2:00 PM

Held: Lawrence County Fairgrounds, Southwest of Bedford, IN

Directions: From the Junction of Hwy 37 and Hwy 50 SOUTH OF BEDFORD, go west on Hwy 50 W for 0.6 miles, turn right into Fairgrounds.

FOOD SERVICE ON GROUNDS

For additional information call:
812-929-5367

Cold water shelling with Jaime Prohaska of Plum island sea cabins!

By Shetan Noir

Please tell us how you became interested in shell collecting?

Oddly enough, it was never really the "collecting" part of shelling that I was interested in.
Don't get me wrong, I have been shelling for years so I have built up quite the collection,
but it was always the "hunt", the possibility of what was under the rock or what could be
around the next bend that fascinated me. And, something even more strange, I never really
liked the beach. I was always a lake person, but during long stays at our summer cottage, I
would collect the empty freshwater mussel shells mixed in with the weeds along the
shoreline. I would collect even the broken pieces. They had a thick layer of iridescent nacre
on the underside. When I held them up to the sky the sunlight would reveal a secret
rainbow that would shimmer and shine. That is my first memory of shell collecting - that's
what got me hooked.

Are there any rules to shell collecting In Massachusetts, like how many or what species you are allowed to keep?

From what I've researched, it depends on what beach you are at. Some beaches are protected by state and federal organizations. Some shell collectors are also rockhounds and bone and/or fossil collectors. Bones, such as whale bones or bones from mammals that are protected under the ESA (Endangered Species Act of 1973), are very protected and it's illegal to remove them from the beach unless you have a special permit.

Is there an etiquette to sea shell or beach treasure collecting?

Yes, one that I am most passionate about is that if you find a shell (no matter how beautiful it is), if there is a living creature inside, return it to the ocean to "shell on" and live happily ever after. Shells that are empty or expired are fair game and ok to take. Also, this is just my own rule, but if you are shelling with kids or a brand new sheller, let them make the finds and keep the loot. It's exciting to make first time finds and when you've been shelling for a while, it's nice to allow people who are new to shelling experience the thrill of it all.

Where and when are the best places and times to collect shells?

To name a few on my bucket list, for warm water shelling, Australia and Hawaii for sure, both places have endemic species meaning they can only be found there. In the US, Sanibel Island is amazing and one of the most desired shelling destinations for shellers in the US. The reason Sanibel is so amazing is because it has such an abundance of shells and also a wide variety of species. The reason for this is where it's positioned and situated in the ocean. For cold water shelling, I often call Plum Island the Sanibel of the north. I call it this because like Sanibel, Plum Island is situated in a similar manner and gets both a wide variety of species as well as an abundance of shells. Not to get too nerdy, but Plum Island also has a very flat and shallow sub-marine floor that allows shells to easily wash up onto the beach. Northern Moon Snail Shells are especially in abundance here as the environment is perfect for them to thrive and in addition their round design allows them to roll right up onto the beach for shellers to find them. The crown jewel of cold water shelling, for me, would be Scotland! I have a trip planned for this June 2023! I am super looking forward to it - can't wait!

The best time to shell varies from warm water shelling and cold water shelling. A shellers rule of thumb is "low tide" and most of the time 2 hours before low tide so that you can shell the outgoing tide. If you wait until it's dead low, then you are then rushing against the incoming tide to collect your shells. 2 hours before low tide is my jam for Plum Island especially. For places like Florida (where there is not a huge tidal variance - average 2 to 3 feet) there is not a huge difference between high and low tide so I'm not so strict. Places like Plum Island have an average of 8 to 9 feet and there is a huge difference in the beach geography from high tide to low tide. For instance in my videos, I often shell "the rocks". Those same rocks during high tide are completely covered with water and can't even be seen. And then there's the Bay of Fundy which has the largest tidal variance in the world - 38 feet - whoa! I've never shelled there, but it's on my list!

I have seen in some of your videos on your youtube channel that you go collecting in the winter time, do you find more shells during the winter storm season?

Yes - from October through March is my most favorite time to shell. The reason is winter storms! Winter storms and Nor'easters really churn up the ocean and kick up a lot of those deep water shells. Deep water shells like Common Whelks, Stimpsoni Colus, New England Neptuned and the Pelican Foot shell are super rare and they don't often make it to shore in one piece. In Florida, shellers are always after the iconic Junonia for this very same reason. I often call the New England Neptune the Junonia of the north. I've never found a fully intact one. It's my bucket list shell for sure.

What are the most common shells you find?

On Plum Island, the most common shells are Atlantic Surf Clams and Quahogs/ hard shell clams. The most common shells I find (that I collect) are Northern Moon Snail Shells. They are an absolute favorite of mine for 2 reasons - size and color variation. So many times you can find a shell and no matter how many times you find it, they almost look exactly the same - identical. Northern Moon Snail shells can be as small as a teeny tiny pebble or as large as a softball. In addition, the colors I've found range from jet black to purple, pink and my most favorite - blue!

What are the rarest shells that you look for?

The New England Neptune is my white whale shell for sure. I've never found a fully intact one. This winter a friend of mine found a fully intact Pelican Foot here on Plum Island. I have *heard* they could be found here, but I didn't believe it until I saw the specimen she found. It was perfect - no breaks - seriously unreal. About a week later another friend of mine found a piece of Pelican Foot - the apex. Even finding a piece of a shell that is that rare is super exciting. A few people I've shelled with have found completely intact New England Neptunes. Even though I didn't find it myself, it's super exciting to be there when one is found.
We all "shell-a-brate" when that happens - shell humor

The moon snail shells you have shown in your videos are impressive. Are those the typical size that show up on the beach?

From my experience, on Plum Island, the typical size is anywhere from 1 inch to 2.5 inches. It's more rare to find ones that are over 3 inches and super rare to find any over 3.5". The biggest I've found here on the island is 4 inches. There are some areas in CA where the environment is so perfect it allows them to grow as large as 5 inches! I would faint if I ever found one that large.

Besides shells, what else do you collect on the beaches?

Beach wood, seaglass, pottery and old bottles are also super fun to find. I really enjoy finding fully intact old bottles. The bottom of the bottles are marked with plant locations, mold numbers and date codes. It's really fun to pull something out of the ocean or the sand and then hit the interwebs to research what it is and what year it was made. It's so fun to be able to find something that hasn't been touched in over 100 years. It really amazes me. It's like finding a little bit of history.

Is there anything else you would like to tell us about shell collecting?

Yes, the beach and shell collecting in general is really helpful for anyone with anxiety or those who have a hard time disconnecting from work or technology. The world is moving so fast and we are always "on". It's nice to be able to go somewhere that you can disconnect for a bit and be fully present and in the moment. I can honestly say that shelling is rare for me in that when I'm shelling, I'm fully present - my mind and body are in the same place at the same time. The ocean, the sounds, the smell of the salt in the air - it's all very therapeutic. If you have a hard time turning off the noise in your life, give shelling and the beach a try.

Do you have any social media sites or a website?

Yes - I have all the social media's and sites:

YouTube:https://www.youtube.com/@PlumIslandSeaCabin

Facebook:https://www.facebook.com/PlumIslandSeaCabin

Instagram:https://www.instagram.com/sea.cabin

Etsy:https://www.etsy.com/shop/PlumIslandSeaCabin

PLUM ISLAND SEA GLASS CABIN

World of Rocks

World of Rock

World of Rocks
42 N. Huron   Ypsilanti, MI
Minerals   Fossils   Jewelry

World *of* Rocks

Crystals   Fossils   Jewelry

32 N. Huron Ypsilanti, MI

Hours
Mon – Fri : 11 AM – 7 PM
Sat : 10 AM – 7 PM
Sun : 12 PM – 5 PM

The Beauty of Sea glass interviewing Mary Beth Beuke

by Shetan Noir

Can you please tell us more about your background?

I am a Pacific Northwest (US) native and have lived and worked along the Oregon and Washington Coasts for over 30 years. I remember being enamored with the ocean and hiking the long shorelines while very young. As a young adult, I grew more serious about trekking and covering as much beach terrain as I had time for. The exercise and beauty I experienced through those challenging hikes got me out into nature, and I began a practice of daily beach litter pickups from along our shores. The beach cleaning naturally merged into a concentration on "treasure hunting" and subsequently, sea glass collecting. Over many years, my sea glass collection emerged and grew, so I began studying its origin and history. I now use my rarest specimens of (West Coast Sea Glass) pieces in fine silver and sterling silver jewelry creations.

(Should we define sea glass here?) Sea glass defined generally includes the small pieces of historic glass that were once thrown "away" into the ocean and have naturally tumbled for centuries, decades and years. Sea glass can originate from an abundance of different sources; common bottles, household containers, glass lampshades, window glass, game pieces, soda pop containers etc. A hundred years ago, before plastics, everything was contained in glass.

WestCoastSeaGlass.com

How did you become interested in collecting sea glass?

My beachcombing friends and I began to travel on sea glass adventures. As we did so, we became more interested as the collection grew and we began to take notice of the different colors, patinas, unique relics and shapes and sizes we found. Visiting different beaches and hiking for the beauty was a main goal but the challenge of finding sea glass quickly became the motive. Now our collection spans over 40 countries as well as a complete Pacific Ocean representation of specimens from Mexico to Kodiak Island Alaska, the Pacific islands, the Salish Sea and more.

What colors do you typically see in sea glass?

Sea glass can be found in just about every color there is. But several colors are very common and there are many colors that are highly rare and sought after by enthusiasts around the world.
Typically, most sea glass hunters have more browns, frosty whites and dark greens in their beach bags than other rarer shades. That is because when the mass produced, industrialization of bottling began, those were generally the most common bottle colors.

Are certain colors more sought after or more rare to find?

Yes! Color, condition, frostiness, certain shapes and even some specific treasures like marbles, bottle stoppers, figural pieces and embossed finds are highly coveted. Over the past couple decades, the popularity of sea glass collecting has resulted in a wave (excuse the pun) of folks vying for the desirable colors like blues, lavenders, yellows, reds and oranges. Years ago, we developed a nice, broad-sweeping color chart that lists in order, the general rarity of the sea glass color spectrum. The chart attached reads like a book; top to bottom, left to right.

Sea Glass Rarity

Turquoise

UV Lime

Olive Green

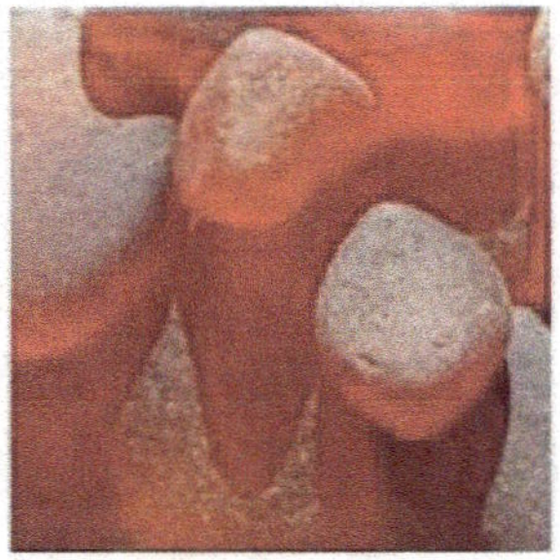

White

Yellow

Grey

Cobalt Blue

Brown

Red

Teal Green

Honey Amber

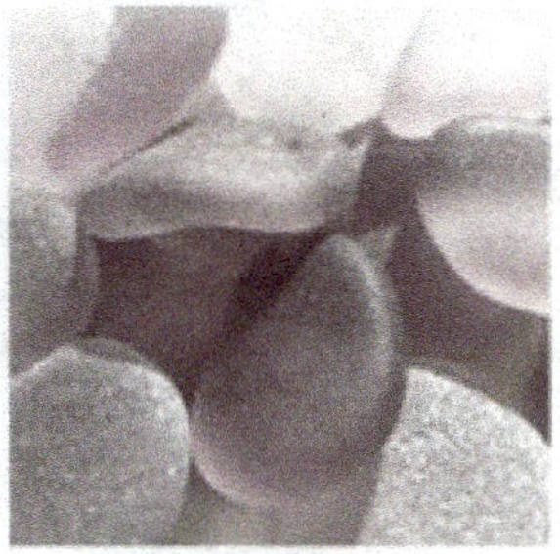

Emerald Green

Orange

Black

Amethyst

Seafoam Green

Pink

Cornflower

Aqua Blue

When and where are the best places and times to find Sea glass?

There are dozens of factors that help point a collector to a successful hunt.

- Check the local tide charts for the beach you'd like to visit.
- Search at low tide and make sure you pay attention to the high tide lines of the beach. Some larger pieces will be dropped by the high tide up there.
- Search in a location where there's older settlement history of communities that would have used glass products decades or centuries ago.
- Shores ajacent to shipping lanes with a history of busy mariner traffic are a great place to look.
- If it's safe, finding a beach near where dumping history occurred can be very helpful.
- The mouth's of rivers where they open up to the sea or lake can sometimes show a concentration of sea glass.
- Rocky shore terrain and pebble washes seem to "hang onto" sea glass more often than wide stretches of sandy beach.

Keep in mind that a "good" sea glass beach can be many different things to many different people. We recently did a survey of over 50 different collectors who rated what they look for most in a good sea glassing location. The answers ranged from "where there's sunny weather", to "where I can find a lot" of sea glass, to "a beach with no other people on it" But most importantly enjoy the beach and help take care of it.

Are there any laws or rules when collecting sea glass? Do you need a permit?

Yes. Beachcombing in general does have regulations. We strongly urge folks when hunting for sea glass to know the local property access rules. Every area is different. But the most important things to heed are:

- Stay off private property unless invited
- Use public access beaches first and access them where indicated
- Never litter, in fact, it's good stewardship to pick up garbage as you beachcomb
- Keep updated on where shoreline preservation and restoration regulations are in effect.
- Sea glass is considered garbage, so it is legal to pick it up almost everywhere.
- Some countries do require a permit to pick up historical relics from beaches.
- Beaches on state park lands may prohibit collecting when the finds are considered a cultural or natural resource.

With all of that said, it is always the best practice to be informed of the regulations in the location of where you are going. And stay safe. Beaches can be hazardous, undulating and difficult to navigate especially during high tide and storms.

How can people determine if the Sea glass is real sea polished gla.ss or machine tumbled?

Sea glass and machine tumbled frosted glass are exceedingly different from eachother. Sea glass is the correct term for glass that has spent time (usually decades) tumbling in a natural body of water. Sea glass has been on a journey and is a product of history. The faux product has really become a problem over the past few years especially as natural sea glass has gained in popularity. With the real deal it's fascinating to wonder, study and discover; Where did it come from originally? How did it get here? How old is it? What human used this long ago and what story might it tell? Machine made "frosted glass" can be pretty but we don't call it sea glass. And yes, some afficanados can tell the difference but it takes an educated and trained eye to recognize the correct frosty surface patina and characteristics of which I term as "how sea glass behaves" when in a natural water environment, with ocean wave action and sandy, or rocky shoreline terrain. Machine tumbled glass is very distinctly a commercialized product that should not be called "sea" glass.

Can you tell us more about your book, Ultimate guide to Sea glass?

Surely! Throughout my past 20+ years or so of collecting, I began to blog and journal about my finds, the colors and the history I researched about the pieces. I began charting my finds, photographing unique treasured pieces, and recording notes on best tide times, weather, sunlight and premium terrain for finding sea glass. One day, a large US publisher phoned me and asked me to write a book. I told them I'd "already been writing it over the past several years". I contracted with them and The Ultimate Guide to Sea Glass was printed a year or two later. It's considered a coffee table book with large, color photos and 260 pages of stories and info.

I saw on your website that there is a North American Sea glass Association, can you tell us more about that organization?

Myself and a handful of sea glass jewelers and enthusiasts from around the country joined together online just over 15 years ago to share our fascination with sea glass. We shared stories, education and even crafting projects with one another We began writing articles for others about the hobby. From there we broadened and deveoped an offical association of which I became a founding board member of. We organized national events about everything sea glass including rarity contests, artisan booths, lectures and featured collections. We are not an international group serving members from around the globe.

Is there anything else you would like to tell us about Sea glass collecting?

The joy of the hunt, the historic "archeaology" aspect, and getting out into nature is really what sea glass collecting it's all about.

Do you have any social media sites or

?Main website full of articles, over 900 listings and pretty photos at WestCoastSeaGlass.com. I sent my social media info in previous email.

Contact Us

Tell us what you're thinking.

INFORMATION

WestCoastSeaGlass@hotmail.com

OFFICE PHONE AND HOURS

(360) 461-9560

Mon. – Fri.
Pacific Time, 10am – 4pm

MAILING ADDRESS

(Not a store location)

123 Mariners Dr.

Sequim, Washington, 98382

The Ultimate Guide to
SEA GLASS

Finding, Collecting, Identifying, and
Using the Ocean's Most Beautiful Stones

Mary Beth Beuke

Foreword by Lisl Armstrong

Warm water shelling with Sharmon Simonetti

By Shetan Noir

Please tell us how you became interested in shell **collecting?**

My first experience finding seashells was during a family vacation to Fort Myers Beach, Florida. We knew we were going to move from New Jersey to Florida, so I planned a vacation at Fort Myers Beach to see if we would like the area. My husband and I would be out on the beach before the sun came up and we would spend hours walking the beach looking for treasures. For the next 3 years as we planned our move, each trip back to Florida meant more seashells and I became more and more interested in them and the creatures that created them.

Are there any rules to shell collecting In Florida like how many or what species you are allowed to keep?

There are, but I follow my own rules. I never take anything living from the beach, including sand dollars, snails or hermit crabs in shells. I never throw creatures back into the water, I place them gently. I remove garbage and try to educate others if I see someone perhaps unaware that they are harming a creature. In the county I live in, it is illegal to remove living animals but there are other places where it's not illegal. I personally think it's cruel.

Is there an etiquette to sea shell or beach treasure collecting?

There actually is! Good shelling etiquette would include giving your fellow shellers lots of space, not crowding people and not plopping yourself directly next to someone who is busy digging or going through a pile. It's nice to kind of cross paths and chit chat, but I try not to stay too close to other people. It's really just common courtesy. If I feel that someone is too close, I will just move a little further away. I think that's probably why I enjoy shelling by myself so much!

Where and when are the best places and times to collect shells?

That has to be the number one question I am asked. And the answer is not very straightforward. First, I would recommend a beach that is known to have seashells. Not all beaches do! Once you have your location sorted out, I would try to visit at low tide. My most favorite time to shell is during low tide and then as the tide is coming in. I feel like it helps push the shells onto the beach. If you don't or can't' visit at low tide, I wouldn't get too upset about it. It's not a science and takes lots and lots of time just walking and looking. If you are not enjoying yourself, you are doing something wrong!

What are the most common shells you find? P

robably the cross-barred venus clam shell and pen shells. They are so common I don't really collect them.

What are the rarest shells that you look for?

Right now the rarest shells I'm hunting for are the cabrit murex, an albino Florida fighting conch and an albino olive. There are plenty of other shells I would love to find and I am always thrilled when I find a "new to me" shell that I've never found before. "The" shell that everyone searches for is the Junonia. I have not found that shell either - yet.

What is your favorite shell to find?

I've been asked what my favorite shell is, and I don't think I can choose just one. However, I absolutely love finding and examining Florida fighting conchs. They can be quite common on some beaches, but each shell is so unique. They can be almost a black color, or bright orange, or a lemony yellow color and they can also have patterns and stripes. I just really enjoy appreciating the attributes of this shell.

Besides shells, what else do you find and collect on the beaches?

In addition to seashells, I also collect sand dollars, urchins, sea fans, and egg casings, which I keep only if the snails inside are not viable. Recently I also had an amazing experience on Sanibel Island, which had been closed for months due to Hurricane Ian. As I was just exploring a very high wrack line I found a single dried up seahorse. I kept looking and I kept finding them. I found 9 in total with 7 of them being completely intact. I was sad they had perished, but I was glad I found them.

Are there any tips you can give us for shell collecting?

I think the best tip I could give would be to have fun. I would hate for anyone to go to the beach and leave disappointed. You never know what's going to be out there!

I thought it was very cool that you also remove trash from the beaches and help wildlife back into the water. It is so important to the ecosystem to do so. What tips would you give people to help clean up the beaches?

I always have extra plastic bags in my backpack when I am walking the beach, just in case someone didn't bring a bag and I see them struggling to carry all their seashells! But I'll also carry one just in case the garbage I'm finding won't fit in my shell bag. I actually pick up trash for the critters, so they don't accidentally eat or ingest something that would harm them. Anyone can do it! Just pick up anything that doesn't belong out in nature and make sure it makes its way to a recycling container or a garbage bin.

Is there anything else you would like to tell us about shell collecting?

I collect shells because the entire experience brings me so much joy. Being out on a beach. Listening to the waves and the shore birds. Seeing a dolphin or a crab scurry by. Picking up seashell after seashell, examining the age, size, quality, specimen - everything about the entire experience is relaxing, fun and enjoyable. I am so fortunate that I get to share my weekly beach walks with people from all over the world on YouTube!

Do you have any social media sites or a website?

 My website is: https://www.swfbeachlife.com/

You can find me on Facebook at:
https://www.facebook.com/southwestfloridabeachlife

I'm also on Instagram:
https://www.instagram.com/swfbeachlife/

But the best place to come along with me and learn about all the fun things that are on the beaches of Southwest Florida is on YouTube:
https://www.youtube.com/@swfbeachlife

Southwest Florida Beach Life (swfbeachlife.com)

Learning about Mudlarking with

Sarah from Manchester Mudlarks

By Shetan Noir

**Hello Sarah from Manchester mudlarks,
Can you tell us what mudlarking is?**

Mudlarking originated in London specifically the Thames where people / children would in the 18th and 19th centuries forage around in the mud of the Thames for items of value to sell . Where as now although the true mudlarks are the Thames mudlarks it's become a term adopted by anyone who looks for treasure along beaches and old landfill sites, fields and tidal rivers . So treasure hunters really but not really looking for things of value but more things of bygone times , interesting pieces of history . A bead has as big a value find wise as does a German marble but not worth any value in money. So yeh hunting for our past really

Why do people go mud larking?

I think people go Mudlarking because it's therapeutic and interesting . Whether it's a walk accross a field eyes peeled or scouring over bottle diggers spoil you always will find something interesting from the past . Something with a story to tell

How did you become involved in mudlarking?

my story starts off as a child in the 70's going bottle digging with my dad . Boy did he dig up some beautiful Victorian items . The bottles were embossed and beautifully coloured . The attention to detail gets you hooked . Fast forward to me in my 50's . Mick skills as a cameraman and editor and my gift of the gab and a hoarding instinct for the old or unusual and away we went .

What kinds of things are you looking for?

We look for anything and everything. I'm known for being a bit of a jam pot hoarder .
Equally as interesting is a half a dolls head . Pipe bowls are always a great find and rarely
you find full pipes or full dolls heads . Buttons ,beads ,bottles there is nothing you don't
look for . The older the better Victorian to 1930's is my preferred era of looking .

How do you find areas to go mudlarking at?

You find some by hard leg work , going for walks and Comparing to old landfill
maps . I found one just looking out the window of the car , I spotted a small bottle
dump in the woods . Walking along streams etc . Plus we get told about places too .

What tools or items do you use while searching for items?

You dont really need much to go Mudlarking . Good wellies if going in streams good boots on bottle dumps . Mudlarkers are generally eyes only although a trowel or scraper may help you retrieve something sticking out of a bank or a spoil pile . A bum bag for your finds maybe a carrier bag for larger finds .

Are there any rules to mudlarking?

Unwritten rules are don't give bottle dump locations away . The diggers are your friends they dig the holes take their bottles and leave us the small unwanted gems , well gems to us . If we told others their sites would get ransacked by diggers ,so no spreading the word on sites . You need a licence to mudlark on the Thames . I have one and it lasts 3 years eyes only no digging on there . To be honest no rules as such for mudlarks outside of the Thames I know you can't sell anything found on the Thames you can gift it but not sell . Oh report any really old finds to local place

What are the most valuable things things you have found?

I don't really find items of value , Mudlarking is definitely not about the worth of items . Frozen charlottes , full dolls heads and limbs , old lined writing slate and slate pencil are bits of nothing but so lovely to find . I did find a spotted dick marble (another larker told me that's what it was) and that is worth about £100 that's the only thing I have a value for and I think probably the only thing worth more than a few pounds lol .

Is there anything else you would like to tell us about mudlarking?

Our you tube channels document our finds and we have a bit of fun along the way . We have tons of regulars that join in the chat on the premiere of our video . I get lots of crafting ideas from viewers and make things out of some of the items I find .. We show our finds on a separate live on a Sunday at 8.30 our videos go out at 7.30 every Saturday . The craft channel is on a bit of a break but will be back soon after a craft room re vamp .we have a Facebook page too. Mudlarking is a great community I get many people saying they can't get out to do these things now and they really feel like we are taking them with us . It's filmed in a way that makes viewers feel apart of the lark . Mudlarking is a little bit more than just finding bits of history it's a thriving little community .

https://youtube.com/@ManchesterMudlarks

https://www.facebook.com/manchestermudlarks

https://youtube.com/@manchestermudlarksgetscraf3574

Pearls of knowledge,
Learning about pearls with
Expert Ashley McNamara

By Shetan Noir

Hello Ashley,

Can you tell us more about your background?I've been fascinated by gemstones and jewelry ever since I was a child. I was a rockhound kid myself, digging for neat looking rocks in my backyard and smashing them open with a hammer to see if I could find any crystals inside – thinking back, I'm lucky I never got any rocks ricocheting in my eyes!

Later in my early 20's I formally joined the jewelry industry when I got my first job working at Kabana Jewelry at the Cherry Creek Mall in Denver, Colorado. They specialized in high-end Australian Opal inlay jewelry and I learned all that I could about these stunning gems.

Later I moved on to working with ABC Gems in the Jewelry District of Downtown Los Angeles. ABC specialized in wholesaling Brazilian Alexandrite, Emeralds, Sapphires and Rubies, and had their own cutting factory in Minas Gerais, Brazil. The owner would come back from Brazil with bags full of newly cut Emeralds, dripping with oil, and I'd get to assist with drying them off, sorting and grading the Emeralds by size and clarity, which I easily could have

spent the rest of my life doing; I find the world of colored gemstones endlessly fascinating!

A little later, I ended up with PurePearls.com, working for the previous owner Amanda Raab. We hit it off immediately, and she sent me to GIA to gain my Pearls Certification, and I've been with Pure ever since!

I initially wasn't a big pearl fan, but as I spent the months and years sorting them, matching pairs, building custom design jewelry for clients and educating people about pearls, I gradually fell in love with their quiet beauty and glow.

How did you become interested in fresh water pearls?

I love Freshwater pearls! Their myriad colors, that subtle glow that comes from within and their durability make them one of my favorite pearl types … in my mind, they are the underdogs of the pearl world, but I don't think they'll stay that way for long with all the advances in pearliculture techniques the Chinese are making. Bead-nucleated Edison pearls with their intense Royal Purple and Magenta colors, the large hollow Soufflé pearls with their electric luster and Orient and Metallic Freshwater pearls are all incredible examples of the leaps and strides

that the world of Freshwater pearls has to offer pearl lovers. It's a very exciting time!

Even with just the cute little Button-shaped Freshwater pearls, you can find this really cool transparency that's visible just under the surface … it's hard to describe to laypeople without being able to show them in real life, but I've noticed that the coolest White Freshwater pearls almost look like milk glass. The industry term for this effect is "water", which tries to describe the transparency of thenacre layers; the tighter and more densely the layers are arranged, the easier time that light has penetrating the crystal and rebounding back to the viewer creating these amazing optical effects unique to pearls, and Freshwater pearls in particular!

Is there a difference between fresh water pearls and salt water pearls?

Yes, definitely! Freshwater pearls are cultured/grown in the Freshwater pearl mussel *hyriopsis cumingii*, which inhabits lakes, ponds and rivers. Of course there are a variety of Freshwater mussel species known throughout the world that can produce pearls, but it's primarily the hybrid *cumingii* mussel farmed in China that is used to culture pearls today.

There are six main saltwater pearl oysters used to culture pearls around the world. Saltwater oysters inhabit oceans and tropical lagoons in all regions.

The Pinctada margaritifera black-lipped pearl oyster grows the famous Black Tahitian (also known as Black South Sea) pearls that can range from 8.0mm through 17.0mm in size, and sometimes even larger! This particular oyster species can attain sizes of a foot in diameter, and is found primarily in the warm, tropical waters around the French Polynesian islands.

The Pinctada maxima oyster creates White and Golden South Sea pearls is also a very large pearl bearing oyster reaching sizes of 12-Inches in diameter. They are traditionally farmed in Northern Australia and the Philippine Islands.Australia is known for farming the Silver-lipped p. maxima oyster, which produces the finest examples of White South Sea pearls with the cleanest colors, largest sizes and glowing luster. The Gold-lipped p. maxima oyster creates the Golden South Sea pearl, and the pearls with the most intense colors (they can range from pale Champagne hues to orangey 24K Gold colors) are farmed in the Philippine

Islands.

Japan farms the Akoya pearl oyster Pinctada fucata martensii, which is the smallest of all pearl producing oysters, topping out at about 6-inches in diameter. The p. martensii pearl oyster is probably the most famous as it was the first pearl oyster used to successfully culture pearls!

Other saltwater oysters are also used to culture pearls, but are less well-known such as pearls from the Sea of Cortez in Mexico, and the black pearls from Fiji produced by J. Hunter Pearls.

What colors are naturally produced by fresh water pearls?

The Freshwater pearl mussel produces pearls in White, Lavender and Peach to Pink naturally. Of course, as mentioned earlier, bead-nucleated Edison pearls and Soufflé pearl colors can get MUCH wilder, with intense Purple and Magenta colors coming onto the markets today.

What do you look for in quality pearls?

I look for nicely symmetrical shapes, clean surfaces without too many inclusions, either a highly reflective surface or a great glow that appears to come from within, and of course that rainbow iridescence shimmering over the pearls' surfaces that we call Orient. I also tend to keep an eye out for unique colors like Purple, Blue, Aquamarine and Peacock, which I find especially attention grabbing.

What shell species produce the best quality pearls?

I think they've all got something special and unique to contribute to the world of pearls – I really couldn't pick one as the "best"!

Can pearls be found in wild shells or are they just produced in human control habitats?

Absolutely! Wild pearl hunters are out there, collecting natural pearls all the time, it's just less talked about because finding natural pearls is a rare occurrence and it's easier for most people wanting pearl jewelry stick with cultured pearls.

Can the people legally harvest pearls from the wild?

Yes, although some countries like Australia and French Polynesia heavily monitor what oysters can be harvested in order to protect their wild oyster populations. My best advice would be to check with any local authority first before going pearl hunting!

Can you tell us more about your business and website?

We specialize in cultured pearl jewelry and source our pearls from pearl auctions and direct from the pearl farmers around the world! We create all of our pearl jewelry from scratch, to order, and we have a blast doing it. I am incredibly honored to be in a positio where I can bring this gorgeous, natural beauty to people all over the world!

Is there anything else you would like to tell us about pearls?

Just keep an eye on the Chinese Freshwater pearl industry – there's some very special advances happening there that are taking the pearl world by storm!

Where can people go to find out more about pearls?

I have spent the last two decades making Pure Pearls the go-to place for Pearl Education, so I'd definitely recommend visiting my site's Education resources for more in-depth information if your readers are interested. For those looking to get expert-tier in learning about

pearliculture, then another fantastic resource is a book called "Pearls" by Elizabeth Strack, who is by far the most knowledgeable person on the subject, and who has taught me almost everything I know. It's a bit expensive but it is one of my most treasured and heavily referenced books in my library!

www.purepearls.com

PURE PEARLS
• QUALITY BY NATURE •

Okemos Location

4738 Central Park Dr. Suite D
Okemos, MI 48864

Hours of Operation
Mon - Fri: 10am - 9pm
Sat: 11am - 9pm
Sun: 11am - 6pm

(517) 749-0710
revlillybeyondadream@gmail.com
www.facebook.com/beyondadreamokemos
www.instagram.com/leeannlillybeyondadream

Brighton Location

300 Brookside Lane, Suite 100

Brighton, MI 48116

Hours of Operation

Mon - Fri: 10am - 8pm

Sat: 10am - 8pm

Sun: 11am - 6pm

(810) 588-6756

beyondadreambrighton@gmail.com

www.facebook.com/beyondadreambrighton

www.instagram.com/beyondadreambrighton

Great Lakes Rocks and Minerals
Michigan Greenstone Chlorastrolite
Hexagonaria Percarinata Petoskey stone
Hematite Amethyst
Jaspelite
Leland Blue
Thomsonite
Fluorecent Sodalite Yooperlite
Copper Replacement Agate
Copper Silver Crystal
Leland Blue
Chlorastrolite
Chlorastrolite, Prehnite, Feldspar, Copper
Copper Replacement Agate
Copper Silver
Lake Superior Agate
Thunderegg
Agatized Honeycomb Coral
Copper Replacement Agate
Chrysocolla
Datolite
Thomsonite
Chlorastrolite
Banded Chert
Datolite
Lake Superior Hurricane Agate
Chlorastrolite with Copper Crystal
Lake Superior Agate
Copper Replacement Agate
Lake Superior Amethyst Agate
Favosites Charlevoix stone
Snowflake Mohawkite
Thunderegg
Unakite
Lake Superior Agate
Petoskey Stone
Chlorastrolite
Lake Superior Eye Agate
Crinoid
Pudding Stone
Lake Superior Agate
Chris Cooper
Trilobite

Rockhound treasure finding along the great lakes shores

By Shetan Noir

**The shores of the great lakes hold a treasure trove of rocks and minerals
For collectors to find.
While Agates and Yooperlites are some of the most sought after, there are many
other interesting stones to seek out while at the shorelines.**

SEPTARIAN NODULES

Sometimes called lighting stones or turtle stones. Septarian Nodules are brown colored
stones with calcite crackles over thier surface.
Giving the stones a lighting like pattern.
**How are theSEPTARIAN NODULES
Formed?**
They are formed as a ball of clay on the ocean floor around 50 million years ago. Over time
the balls of clay cracked and the cracks were filled in with a white to yellow Calcite.
The great lakes area were once under a great ocean and the fossil remains of the corals can
still be found along the shorelines to this day

Hag stones

Hag stones are beach stones with natural holes through them.

FOLKLORE

According to folklore the hag stones are said to have magical powers, its said that if you find a hag stones it will bring you luck, good health and protection while locking bad luck and negative energy away from you.

Leland blues stones or slag glass

The blue slag pieces found on Vans Beach near Leland Michigan are very popular for jewelry making. Produced from industrial slag that was once dumped into the lakes. The Leland blue stones are broken up during winter storms and washed ashore.

There are many areas around the great lakes that have slag deposits. The slag can range in color from teal blue to black but always has a glassy look to it.

Unakite

This brightly colored green and peachy orange stone is a standout on the beach.
Unakite is comprised of pink feldspar, green epidote, and clear quartz.
It is also called Epidote Granite.
This one is said to be semi-precious.
Unakite is believed to help with emotions.

Petoskey stones

The Petoskey stone is fossilized pre-historic coral fossilized rugose coral, Hexagonaria percarinata.
The hexagon pattern covering the fossil becomes more details once polished.

PUDDING STONES

Pudding stones are a type of sedimentary rock known as a conglomerate. Michigan's pudding stones are conglomerates that have been metamorphosed into a metamorphic rock called quartzite..
Pudding Stones form from varying sizes of sediment (sands, usually) and pebbles. Smaller sands or silts surround larger pebbles and harden deep beneath the Earth's surface. In the case of pudding stones, they are first formed from sand that is then metamorphosed into quartzite under heat and pressure.

Michigan Greenstone
The state gemstone of Michigan, ischlorastrolite, a variety of the mineral pumpellyite. It also goes by the common name of greenstone or Isle Royal greenstone.
It can only be found and collected in the kewanaw peninsula of upper Michigan.
No collecting from Isle Royale can be legally done.
The small green pebbles look best when polished.

GLR&M
GREAT LAKES
ROCKS & MINERALS
Join us on
Facebook !

The Livingston Gem and Mineral Society
48th Annual
ROCKHOUND'S DREAM SHOW
Sat. Sept 16 & Sun. Sept 17, 2023
Sat. 10-6 Sun. 10-4

Hosting the 82nd. Convention of the Midwest Federation of Mineralogical & Geological Societies!

Livingston Gem and Mineral Society
LGMS

ROCKS-FOSSILS -CRYSTALS-
UNIQUE JEWELRY

GEM AND MINERAL DEALERS

SILENT AUCTION
CLUB TABLE
CHILDRENS TABLE
DEMONSTRATIONS

MID WEST FEDERATION

LAPIDARY DISPLAYS
FLOURESCENT ROCKS
WIRE WRAPPING
SILVERSMITHING

Hartland Educational Support Service Center (Old Hartland High School)
9525 E. Highland Road, Howell, Michigan 48843
Admission: adults $5.00, 12-18 years $1.00, under 12 years free

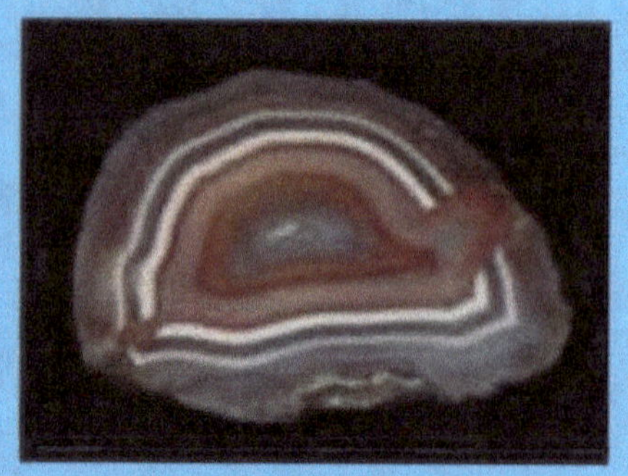

Concessions Available
More Information: Ed Oller (810) 241-8801 or Lori Irvin (810) 820-0494

livingstongems.com

Like us on facebook
Livingston Gem and Mineral Society

Livingston Gem and Mineral Society presents The Rockhound's Dream Show 2023

48th Annual Show - Sept. 16 - 17

Hosting the 82nd Convention of the Midwest Federation of Mineralogical & Geological Societies

Come Enjoy the Fun!

September 16th - 10am-6pm
September 17th - 10am-4pm

Hartland Educational Support Service Center
9525 E. Highland Rd.
Howell, MI 48843

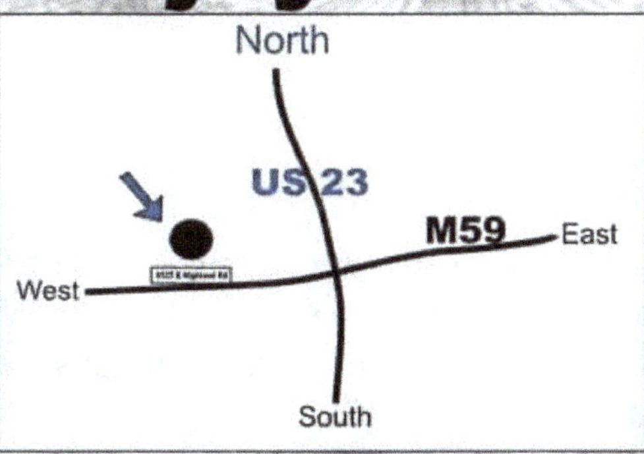

Concessions Available

Admission:
$5 Adults, 12-18 $1, under 12 Free

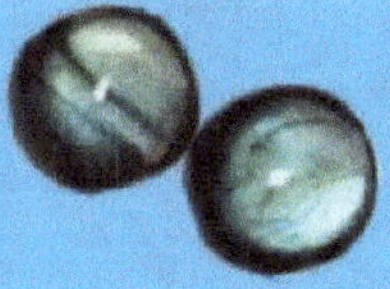

Silent Auctions & Drawings

ROCKS - CRYSTALS - JEWELRY - SPECIMENS/FOSSILS - DECORATIVE ITEMS

Diverse Vendors	**Michigan Specimens**
Lapidary Displays	**Club Table**
Fluorescent Rocks	**Kids' Table**
Jewelry Creations	**Rock Slabs**

Tour the LGMS Workshop for Demos   **livingstongems.com**
Facebook - Livingston Gem and Mineral Society

Agate hunting

by Shetan Noir

Northern Great Lakes area-Agates, the beautiful colorful gem stones of Lake superior and the great lakes state. These different sized and colored gemstones are scattered across Wisconsin, Minnesota and Upper Michigan. While many rock hounds find and collect these beauty's on the shores of Lake superiors there are a lots of places to stop and look for agates.

For the Agate lovers and rock hound enthusiasts here is a small list of places to take road trip too and collect agates. When Agate collecting look stones with a waxy, glossy surface which had bands and some translucency.Lake shores and gravel pits are your best bet for sites But get permission first before entering the gravel pits.

Minnesota

Guides to rock collecting in Minnesota

http://dnr.state.mn.us/geologyrec/index.html

http://files.dnr.state.mn.us/lands_minerals/recgeo.pdf

rst stop, The Moose Lake state park where you can view many different Agates and read about how the agates are rmed.

oose Lake State Park

ocated 1/4 miles east of I-35 at the Moose Lake exit #214. The park entrance is off County Road 137. Take the Moose ke exit off I-35. Then go east on County Road 137 until you see the park signs about 1/2 mile down the road.

ours

ril- Memorial Day: Tuesday-Saturday 9-4 intermittently. May: 9-4 7 days a week, Memorial Day- Labor Day: nday-Wednesday 9-4, Thursday 9-7, Friday and Saturday 9-9. Labor day through November office open termittently 9-4 seven days a week.

tp://www.dnr.state.mn.us/state_parks/moose_lake/index.html

oose Lake area chamber of commerce

u will need to stop in here and buy your agate collecting permit and map.

24 Arrowhead Lane

O. Box 110

oose Lake, MN 55767

18) 485-4145

00) 635-3680

tp://www.mooselakechamber.com/agate-picking-permit.php

here is also the annual Agate days celebration in july.

he North shore Drive route along Minnsota's Hwy 61 in Cook County.

here are several road side parks along the lake superior shore line that provide excellent places to rock collect. Agates, uartz and amethyst are just a few of the treasure that can be found id you are willing tospend the time.

he beaches of Lutsen-Tofte-Schroeder, Grand marais, Grand portage are all good spots.

isconsin/Michigan border

tp://wisconsingeologicalsurvey.org/

tp://www.gatorgirlrocks.com/state-by-state/wisconsin.html

ittle girl Point, Ironwood, Gogebic county Michigan

tp://gogebic.org/forestryandparks_littlegirlspoint.htm

Michigan's Upper peninsula

Ontonagon, Gitche Gumee Landing Michigan

UNION BAY
Highway M-107 winds along the Lake Superior shore at Union Bay. Miles of beach provide an area for swimming, sunsets, and agate hunting. Inquire locally to find out just what an agate looks like. Copper specimens can also be found among the pebbles, broken from rock brought in to prevent erosion of the highway

http://lakegogebicarea.com/area-information/gogebic-ontonagon-county-information/

Grand marais, Mi

The owner of Gitche Gumee Agate and history museum is an expert at finding Agates and offers workshops on finding them.

E21739 Braziel Street,

Grand Marais, MI 49839

(906) 494-3000

Scenic routes along the northern shores of the Upper Michigan's peninsula provide many beaches to stop at and stretch your legs as you look for agates.

http://www.michigan.org/blog/guest-blogger/six-scenic-drives-for-pure-michigan-summer-road-trips/

Good luck and have fun, hunting Agates.

https://www.facebook.com/joy.bec19

rebecca.ellul@yahoo.com
Or
whitehouse.wilcox@yahoo.com

MAX
UV
YOOPERLITES MAX UV
W-I-D-E BEAM & LOADS OF POWER!
NEW RELEASE

LIGHT UP THE NIGHT
YOOPERLITES
WWW.YOOPERLITES.COM

LIGHT UP THE NIGHT
YOOPERLITES

Now accepting
Articles

ROCK HOUND AND PROSPECTORS MAGAZINE

Call for Articles
About
Rock hounding, Fossil collecting
Gem, rock, or mineral specific articles
Gold or precious metals prospecting
How-to articles and/or DIY articles
Mining locations open to the public
Gem and fossil shows, expos or stores

Articles lengths should be 700 to 2500 words

Send submissions to
rockhoundmagazine@yahoo.com

Writers will
Receive 1 pdf
Copy of magazine

62nd ANNUAL
GEM,JEWELRY,BEAD,ROCK &
MINERAL SHOW
JUNE 2, 3 & 4 2023
Friday   Noon – 6 pm
Saturday   10 am – 6 pm
Sunday   11 am – 4 pm
Admission
Adults $4, Seniors & Students $3
Children under 12 Free
Fulton County Fairgrounds
Junior Fair Building
8514 SR 108
Wauseon, Ohio
North of the Ohio Turnpike
Exit 34
State Line Gem & Mineral Society
Website http://statelinegms.com
GEODES!
CLASSES!
THE STATE LINE GEM & MINERAL SOCIETY

Summer Rock Swap

Beer Family Farm

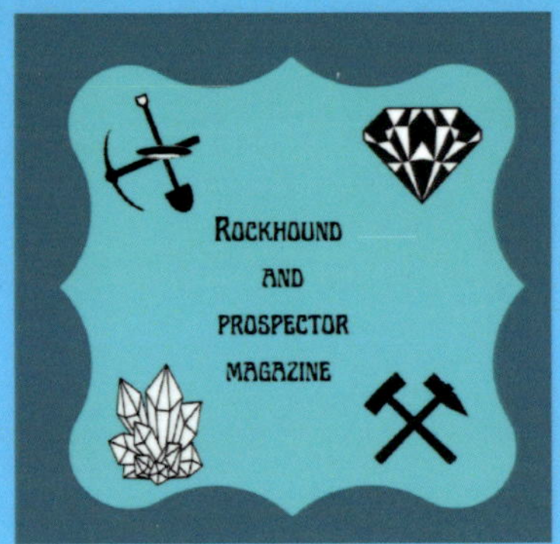

spring 2023

ISBN 9798397013932

The Complete Guide to Home Remedies for Gout:

Omotayo Obi

From Kitchen to Cure